THE UNIVERSE TALKING

Anecdotes from an ordinary life - How to recognise that the Universe is on your side

Linda Rowntree
Intuitive Life Coach-Psychic Medium-Spiritual Guide

THE UNIVERSE IS TALKING TO YOU

Copyright© 2021 by Linda Rowntree

All rights reserved. No part of this publication may be reproduced, stored in a retrieval system or transmitted, in any form or by any means, electronic, mechanical, photocopying, recording or otherwise, without permission in writing from the author, except in the case of cited, brief quotations embodied in critical reviews.

About the Author

Linda was born and brought up in the heart of the Suffolk countryside and so has a strong connection with Nature and all that it brings.

Her career as a Corporate Accounts Manager was cut short after a car accident and she then retrained to be a Complementary Therapist, eventually giving up a well-paid career to run her own business.

Having seen spirit as a young child it is no surprise that in the last few years Linda has once again embraced her connection and is now a successful businesswoman running the Rainbow House Wellbeing Centre in the pretty market town of Sudbury, Suffolk.

Her career has taken her through many twists and turns but it has been her intuition and deep innate belief in Universal Law that has made any transformation easier and has enabled her to make choices and decisions with confidence.

Linda is a successful Psychic Medium, Intuitive Life Coach and Spiritual Guide connecting with people to help empower them to transform their lives.

'I was given the name 'Spiritual Guide' in a trance circle I sat in many years ago. I thought it a bit odd at the time as I saw it as a job rather than a name, and a job for those that had passed over and who had much more of a higher level of Spiritual awareness.

However, early in 2021, I was given the name again by a student who said that I was his 'Spiritual Guide'. This brought back the memory of my time in Waltham Abbey and the Trance Medium Andy who channelled the name back then. All those that sat in that circle were given a spirit name one evening and although I still remember the evening, I had not taken it literally so let it slip away from me. I have since travelled my life path wherever it has taken me and reconnected with my Soul Purpose.

Right here and right now, I am prepared to step into 'Spiritual Guide' whether that is in name, title, or occupation. I now embrace it wholeheartedly.

Dedications

"How do you spell LOVE?" asked Piglet
"You don't spell it, you feel it" replied Pooh"

A. A. Milne

This book is dedicated to my Mother – who has helped me enormously since she passed to Spirit.

Neville, a friend who has been back often with love, affection and a wicked sense of humour.

To my brother Tony whom I have never met, but look forward to meeting when my time comes.

To my Father – a true inspiration to everyone who met him, and who I miss every single day. Until we meet again.

To my friends and long-suffering family for their encouragement and support, they have always been there for me and for that I shall be eternally grateful.

To Carrie Parkin of Virtually Balanced - who helped me to publish this book. She is my highly recommended Virtual Assistant www.virtuallybalanced.com and another believer in the magic.

TABLE OF CONTENTS

About The Author iii

Dedications v

Foreword vii

The Magic For Me ix

Section One – What The Magic Is 1

Section Two – The Magic Is Real 8

Section Three - Other People's Magic 68

Section Four - And Finally 77

Foreword

"Grown men can learn from very little children for the hearts of the little children are pure. Therefore, the Great Spirit may show to them many things which older people miss"

Black Elk – Oglala Lakota Sioux (1863-1950)

I have been told over the past few years and by several people that I should and will write a book, something which I have felt is in me too. That being the easy part, knowing what to write about the more difficult part. I knew that it would be a book, but not a book. This puzzled me at first because what is a book if not a book? I knew it wouldn't be a biography, that is for another time. I knew that it would help others, but it wouldn't be a manual as such.

I know a bit about this and a bit about that like most people, but nothing seemed to thrill me with inspiration… until one day my eldest Granddaughter wanted to learn about magic. Being only five I tried to explain to her that the slight of hand she had been watching at the time on the television was an illusion and not real magic. She then asked me what 'real magic' was and I explained to her that the Universe is full of magic if we only see the signs and embrace the experiences when they happen. I then related a couple of the stories to her which I have included in this book.

Since then, we have found our own magic between us and on many occasions and I shall always cherish those experiences especially.

The title for this book was originally 'Rainbow Magic' which comes from my company name and home 'Rainbow House'. If you have ever seen and felt the wonder and excitement of such a spectacle - a rainbow is the magic of nature itself – you may start to understand why I had intended to call this book 'Rainbow Magic'. However, as I progressed with the book, I realised that it needed a title that spoke directly of what was actually happening. The magic of communication and the Universe's need to communicate with us all.

The question now is where to start?

The Magic for Me

"Those who don't believe in magic will never find it"

Roald Dahl

Magic to me is when people, situations, information, and circumstances come together to create a 'moment', a magical moment which is received and given in a place of truth, love, and respect.

This book which is not a book gives you some idea on how to realise and experience the magic for yourself. With simple instructions to encourage the right frame of mind and general receptivity.

This book, which is not a book, includes a series of anecdotes about such moments. These magical moments I am sure are there for everyone, if you only believe and take the time to recognise them as something special.

Some call these magical moments – synchronicity – but however you choose to perceive them at the time, you just know and do not question that something special has happened. It is in that moment of 'knowing' of peace, truth and love that any such magic thrives.

I do not advocate that you live your life in such moments… well not every day anyway… and if you really need permission for whatever you are asking for confirmation on, then I can think of no better way of seeking that confirmation and enjoying the comfort and joy that it brings.

SECTION ONE – What the Magic is

"Today and everyday – if you are centred in the truth of what your Soul wants, all kinds of magical things happen in favour of synchronicity"
James Redfield

Synchronicity

The word Synchronicity - its origins in sync – meaning to bring together and chronos – meaning time. It can be said then that Synchronicity is the bringing together in time. Time is not linear as we know it, we have a perception of it, and it is relative to our experience of it.

When we experience synchronicities, it is the Universe bringing us help and guidance in the moment, all we have to do is listen and be guided. A synchronous moment will always show itself in perfect timing.

Spiritual Help

The Universe only wants you to be happy and is trying to communicate a willingness to give you everything you want, need, and deserve. This willingness to show you that you are listened to, can be experienced through intuition, signs, coincidences, and synchronicities. These may stretch your imagination at times but rest assured; start recognising the signs and they will appear more frequently, and you will feel more secure.

Everything is energy and vibration, so it is important to keep your own energy as clean and positive as possible. This gives you easier access to experiences and understanding of subtle influences.

The Universe doesn't hear what you say, it hears what you mean and will only give you what you need rather than what you want. Remember everything is vibration and it is vibration that resonates with the Universe. So, if you ask for something and you do not receive it, then it may be because you subconsciously believe that you do not deserve it.

ACTION – Sit peacefully at times to clear and still your mind. Your mind is very powerful and generates its own energy. It also helps to open your mind and imagination. Imagination does not mean that you make things up, just that you have the ability to form new ideas, images or concepts not yet present in your current knowing.

ACTION – You can take this to another level and try your hand at meditation. Meditation has so many benefits, not only for the mind, but for a healthy body, emotional and spiritual state.

ACTION – Daydreaming is a must… the more you use your imagination in this way, the more you will attract what you are daydreaming about. There is a freedom in daydreaming too. It is like we give ourselves permissions that we cannot allow ourselves in the cold light of day. Permission to imagine what we really want… and for the Universe to bring it in whatever way it needs to bring it to us. The Mind loves the images that you give it, and so too does the Universe.

It also helps to feed into the image with the emotion that it brings. Peace, joy and happiness are always good to start. Let your heart guide you here, as your heart is another part of you that will only tell you the truth and only wants what is best for you. If it is a negative emotion, remember too that emotions are energy in motion, and they are on the move for a reason.

> *"If you can hold it in your head, you can hold it in your hand"*
> Bob Proctor

Be willing and open to receiving the signs you have asked for as confirmation. It is more obvious to ask for a specific sign, but other subtle hints are just as valuable. So, the next time you see or hear from someone you have just been thinking about… or you hear the word that has just popped into your head a moment earlier… or when plans go awry and yet there is a hidden benefit in the situation, please recognise it and accept that you are being looked after. You can always take things a step further and ask, 'What is the Universe trying to communicate to me?'

If you do not ask you do not get.

Practical Help

The best way to understand how and when the Universe is communicating with you is to keep a record of what you are asking for, if you are asking. Or just keep a record of things that 'happen' for you or reassure you.

ACTIONS - you can take to help make the magic

- Buy yourself a journal. I find this invaluable in being able to document those magic moments.

- Make an effort to choose a journal specifically for the task in hand. Your journal can be a notebook and some of these already come with inspirational words on the front.

- Dedicate the book to whatever specific purpose you have chosen it for. In this case you may want to write something like... This journal is dedicated to the magic that the Universe brings to me every day. This shows intention for you to take action, but it also shows that you are trusting the Universe to come up with the goods.

- Log each time you ask a question with the date, time and what has been asked for.

- Now, and this is sometimes the difficult bit, let it go. Let any idea of it coming your way and how it should come to you, go completely out of your mind, and get on with your daily routine.

- If you have set a time limit for your sign to come to you, you can check in then… or if you receive the answer before the time is up, make a note of the time and the way in which your answer was presented… by this I mean, did you hear it, did you see it and what were the circumstances surrounding your answer.

A typical example may look like…

August 15th 2019 at 9.15 am – Today I have asked for confirmation that if I am to… tomorrow, then bring to me… before I go to bed tonight. I will take the fact that I do not have… brought to me that I will not… tomorrow. I give thanks now for the answer because I know it will come.

August 15th 2019 at 2.45 pm – I received the sign I was asking for. It came to me as I was… it was truly magical. I am thankful and grateful for this communication.

Whatever happens, trust and believe that the Universe has your best interests at heart even if the message isn't immediately understood.

ACTION – Sit with Nature

It is simple, costs nothing and can bring enormous benefits, physically, mentally, emotionally and spiritually. It is natural so no artificial preservatives or colourings LOL…

The more you sit with Nature, or walk if you prefer, the more you will start to notice the cycles of life, death and rebirth. The natural processes that all life has to go through. This can further enhance the connectedness that we all need to feel. The wonder of insects, birds and animals going about their daily lives with no effort, just going with the flow.

Nature gives us everything we need, food, clothing, shelter and medicine along with awe inspiring views - magical moments to be treasured. We only have to seek to find. It looks after it's own in the best way possible without the need for anything artificial.

On a physical level, we get fresh air, natural light, water, food and medicine. On a mental level it can be very calming to an overactive mind. Emotionally it can bring about a sense of peace, joy and centredness to ease heart felt pain, replacing it with love for who you are, and what the world has to share. From a spiritual perspective, all you need to remember can be found in Nature and completes the cycle for Soul reconnection.

We need the Planet and Nature more than they need us, so be mindful, respectful and enjoy what they give, giving thanks and gratitude for all that you receive.

So, go ahead and ask your question. Be clear on your intention and what you are asking, detach from it, be patient and wait for the answer. Don't get involved with the details, it is not for you to decide when, how etc., that is for the Universe to decide. However, when it does come recognise it for what it is and accept what is being given and in the way it is being given. Do not ignore it either. The Universe understands the bigger picture and has no hidden agenda so have faith. It doesn't hear what you say, it hears what you mean.

Remember when I said that everything is vibration.

"Trust and Believe in yourself as you Trust and Believe in The Universe
The Universe will Trust and Believe in You"
Linda Rowntree

As you read this book you will understand that the sign, answer or whatever you are asking for can come in countless ways.

By documenting these moments, you will see that you do in fact receive information, support and what you need on a regular basis and that these moments will happen more and more regularly. You may even receive magic without really asking for it.

After every encounter, receive the gift gracefully and give thanks for the wonder that you are part of, a truly awesome world and universe.

Happy journaling

SECTION TWO – The Magic Is Real

"Just for today do not worry
Just for today do not anger
Honour your Parents, Teachers and Elders
Earn your living honestly
Show Gratitude for every living thing"
Dr Mikao Usui

Reiki Attunement Magic – For Me

I was driving into work one morning. My daughter was with me as I was dropping her off at College, and we were sitting in traffic as usual. My thoughts were wandering which is also usual and I suddenly asked her 'If I left my body to medical science, do you think they would pay me now?' It may have been too early in the day for her, but she replied, 'For goodness sake Mother no-one else has this kind of conversation with their daughter!' I went on further to explain to her that we had not long moved, and she could do with some new bedroom furniture and as I was a bit strapped for cash at the moment and having nothing to sell or pawn, thought this was a reasonable way out. She didn't answer and so my thought went out to the Universe for a little bit of money which if it came my way wouldn't be wasted... I didn't know at this stage who or what I was putting the request out to and I didn't for one moment think that it would be answered.

However, a few days later I was again on my way to work when the car in front of me braked suddenly. I managed to stop, but the car behind me did not and ran straight into the back of my car. The lady in the car behind didn't brake so hit my car at whatever speed she was going at the time, writing her new BMW off, buckling the boot of my car, but more seriously than that causing me severe damage to my lower spine. My foot had been on the brake and so the bottom half of my body did not move, but the top half was jolted forward tearing the ligaments and tendons around my vertebrae. To cut a long story short I had to have physiotherapy for months, but I was also awarded a substantial amount of money as compensation. My daughter got her bedroom furniture, and I got a new car.

The Universe had answered my call, but not in the way that I had expected or wanted but it most definitely was in the way I needed, even though I was not aware of this at the time.

The original thought which I put out not only gave me what I asked for – the extra money – but went on to change my life completely.

A little while after the accident my daughter and I went to a Mind Body Spirit fair in Colchester and it was touch and go whether I went at all as I was in considerable pain and only just able to drive for short distances. Anyway we went and as I was walking round the hall, a man stepped out in front of me and said 'You look like you are in pain, I am a Healer, may I try and help you?' I was quite embarrassed and muttered 'No thanks I am fine' to which he replied ' I really feel like I can help you, it won't cost you a penny just a few moments of your time and I promise I will not touch you' I looked at my daughter and she said ' What have you got to lose?' So, I sat down.

He was as good as his word, he did not touch me, but the heat I felt was amazing, not from the outside, but from the inside. After about 10 minutes he finished the healing and the result was incredible. I had no pain, could stand up straight and move with ease. His advice was to have sessions of healing as and when necessary because I had responded so positively. The man was a Spiritual Healer, and this was my first experience of non-conformist healing of any sort. I quickly caught up with my daughter who thought it weird.

Jessica, my daughter, was at the time a teenager, and if she couldn't see it, it didn't exist, or at least that was all she was prepared to admit to!

We carried on further round the hall. I do enjoy frozen fresh fruit yoghurts and so my daughter and I sat eating and enjoying the yoghurts. Opposite to where we were sitting was a man doing Reiki healing. He was quite self conscious and moved clumsily, until he was actually giving a treatment and then his whole persona changed. His body moved easily and effortlessly, and I have always referred to his movements as 'poetry in motion'. It was beautiful to watch. As soon as he had finished a treatment, he went back to being rather clumsy and self conscious – this is only my interpretation of what I was seeing at the time, and I am sure he will not mind me referring to him in this way.

During the following week I went into work and felt well enough to walk into town at lunch time, something I had not been able to do since the car accident. On one of these walks, I noticed in a street that I had been along nearly everyday for seven years…. an open door and I could see lots of leaflets and brochures and so, being intrigued I went inside. It turned out to be a spiritual centre and the leaflets were for classes and workshops to do with complementary medicine and all things spiritual.

One leaflet in particular caught my eye, and it was for Reiki Attunements and the catch line for Reiki I was 'good for recharging your batteries and for self-healing'. I was still buzzing from the weekend and grateful that the healing was still working, so much so that I had been able to stop taking the pain killers, something which I hated doing anyway. I wanted to help myself too because I did not like asking for help. So, information in hand I went back to work and rang the number on the leaflet and booked myself on the next Reiki I Attunement in two weeks time.

Reiki I day arrived, and I was a little nervous as at that time I was quite shy and reserved. But I went along and lo and behold, who should be the Reiki Teacher, but the very man I had been watching at the Mind Body Spirit fair a couple of weeks before. It was all seeming to be quite strange.

Reiki I was very subtle for me, no bright light, no aha moment. What it did over the next few months was put things into perspective for me and I realised that I did not want to be a corporate accounts manager for the rest of my working life.

That decision was easy. The difficult part was then deciding what I did want to do. I had a mortgage, was a single parent with responsibilities, and so could not just give my job up and do something different. Again, the thought went out – if I do not carry on with my career, what should I do?

It wasn't long before that question was answered too, and a brochure came through my door for a Reflexology course starting in the New Year in Colchester. I had been toying with the idea of doing something like Aromatherapy or Reflexology and this seemed to be the answer I was looking for and so I enrolled. I have to say at this point that I did not request any such brochure and that the only thing I could think was that I put my name to something or gave my details to someone at the Mind Body and Spirit fair. What a turning point that accident had been.

A year later I was a qualified Reflexologist and looking for more strings to add to my newly honed bow. Course after course came along, I just could not get enough.

Reiki II Attunement was a massive clearing out for me. I had a chest infection, Pharyngitis and a cough which lasted nearly six weeks. Issues which I had thought may come up with Reiki I didn't, but they did with Reiki II – I now realise that I did not have the skills to deal with them before I did my Reiki II.

Reflexology gave me a lot of confidence although at this time I was still guarded. I remember my Reflexology Tutor saying at the end of the course that I was the only student that he knew next to nothing about even after ten months of study together.

Reiki III Attunement was magical in a different way. It was a glorious weekend in August 2002. The sun was shining on the Saturday as I drove to Polstead, a little village in Suffolk and when I got there Marcus my Reiki Master told me that we would be doing the Attunement in another village called Wormingford. This was about twenty minutes' drive from Polstead.

We pulled up off the road alongside the church yard and the view across the valley was breathtaking. As I stepped from the car, a dragonfly came right up to me and hovered. It was beautiful. We walked to the church and through the church yard and out over a stile along a public footpath. The path goes down after a few yards here and into a coppice of trees and then up again into a field. We walked through this field and over the brow of a hill and there was a ring of tree stumps. The tree stumps were where we were going to be doing the Attunement. It could not have been better for me as I love being in nature as I was born and brought up in the Suffolk countryside.

As we settled to do the Attunement. I noticed three swallows flying around the tree stumps. Marcus asked me to sit on one of the stumps and as I did so and closed my eyes, I heard Marcus say something in Japanese and then in English 'The three lost souls', obviously referring to the three swallows. The Attunement over, I asked Marcus what he had said in Japanese which meant the three lost souls. Marcus replied that he had not said anything the whole way through the Attunement and did not know what I was talking about. Another piece of Magic?

We stayed a while and did some tree hugging as the stumps were only part of the landscape here, then we made our way back to the car. Just as we got to the coppice of trees before the churchyard, I was startled by another Dragonfly. We walked to the stile and crossed into the church yard and very soon we were back at the car. There flying round my car door was the Dragonfly from earlier.

Later that evening after I returned home, I was living in Halstead at the time, I had to walk into town to get a bank statement and on my way back as I was walking up the lane which ran at the bottom of my drive; I was amused to see a lady step to one side as if something was in her way. The lady had reached the part of the lane adjacent to my gate and as I drew near to see what had stopped her in her tracks, she declared 'Well I never, fancy seeing a Dragonfly here in the lane' We both admired it and I had to smile to myself as this was the third one I had seen that day.

I had left the top part of our back door open, it was a stable door, as it was such a glorious evening and I was only out for a few minutes. When I opened it to come back into the house, there were three cats sitting eating at my cats' bowl of food.

That was my third lot of three… dragonflies, swallows, and cats. Interestingly it was representative of the insects, bird, and animals. The ultimate magic 3x3!

To recap, the change the accident brought about for me was immense, retraining to change my career path and then my whole outlook on life pushing me towards the Spiritual person I am and always have been.

I would probably still be working in the corporate world or at least it may have taken me a little longer to make the move to be where I am today, if I had not asked the Universe for help and it answered.

"Reiki is Love
Love is wholeness
Wholeness is balance
Balance is well-being
Well-being is freedom from dis-ease
Remember these words for they represent what is Reiki"
Dr Mikao Usui

Reiki Attunement Magic – for others

I was giving a Reiki I Attunement at home and I lived in a mid - terrace property at the time. The gardens were long and narrow, and my garden had fencing on both sides and a 12 foot wall at the bottom. There is another garden and house on the other side of the brick wall and houses either side of mine. Any fields are at least a mile away and so you can imagine our surprise when we heard and then saw a male pheasant strutting down the path towards the house. Clearly a sign not for me, but the two men who I was attuning that day.

On a Reiki III Attunement the lady concerned was more than a little surprised to see a Squirrel peering at her through the open French doors which led into the garden. I had never seen a Squirrel in the garden before and have never seen one since.

On another Reiki I Attunement we could hear squealing from the garden and when I checked I could see a neighbour's cat had cornered something behind a plant pot. The plant pot was up against my house and alongside the dividing fence. I scared the cat away and after a few seconds a little red and white face peered out from behind the pot. It was the most adorable face of a Stoat. After making sure the cat had left, I came in and after a few moments the Stoat ran across the garden and away.

None of these animals I felt were for me, but for the people that I was attuning… even though I loved the experience of each encounter.

As well as having a Totem animal which is with you from birth, you can have an animal that can come and go with messages and guidance which you may need and are significant in the moment.

*"If nothing ever changed
There would be no Butterflies"*
Anonymous

Butterfly Magic

We moved into our terraced house in September 2001… 9/11 to be exact. The following summer my husband had been tasked with re-landscaping the garden. He had strict instructions on what to do and enlisted the help of my father. The day came for work to begin and it was a glorious summer day, warm with a gentle breeze. I was going out with a friend to do some shopping, but before I went, I nipped into the garden to let my husband and my father know that we were leaving and roughly what time we would be back. I noticed a butterfly flying around them both and when I drew near saw that it was a Painted Lady and I remember thinking how appropriate as my mother had been just that… always very smart and well turned out with shoes and handbag matching the outfit she was wearing. My mother passed to the Spirit World the previous November.

When my friend and I returned from our shopping trip I again went into the garden to see how things were progressing and again noticed the Painted Lady butterfly. It only seems special because they do not seem to be as common as they were when I was growing up and in fact it had been several years since I had seen one at all.

A couple of weeks later, I was expecting my husband home for lunch with our youngest daughter and eventually rang to see where they were, only to find out that they had stopped off on the way home and were having lunch already.

As it was such a lovely day and the garden was still under construction, I thought I would take the book I was reading and go to the local park to read it. Just as I set off however, I changed my mind and headed for the cemetery and although it is probably not everyone's ideal place to sit and read a book, I have always found them to be peaceful and there is usually a fair bit of wildlife in them too.

Anyway, I arrived and sat on a bench which was probably about 10 - 12 feet away from my Mother's grave and began reading my book. The back of the bench was against a short hedge and so was quite sheltered. I had been reading for only a few minutes when a butterfly flew in front of me and as I put my book into my lap to watch it, the butterfly flew towards me and touched my right cheek and then flew and sat on my mother's headstone. You guessed it. It was a Painted Lady butterfly!

Interestingly the Ancient Greek word for Butterfly is Psyche which also means Soul and the Ancient Greeks believed that a Butterfly is a Soul looking for its next incarnation.

"Weeds are flowers too – once you get to know them"
A A Milne

My Garden Magic

As well as the magical animals appearing in my garden as described in the anecdotes above, there have been several other incidences where unusual animals and birds have been drawn to it, and these are some of the more memorable, not just for me but for others too.

My daughter and her family were visiting one Sunday afternoon when we heard a screeching from the garden. When we looked, we saw a Peregrine Falcon on the path with a bird in its claws. It stood there for several minutes before taking itself off to the bottom of the garden to finish off it's dinner only leaving a few feathers.

On another occasion I was sitting in the garden and something caught my eye and there sitting on the trellis were two Spotted Woodpeckers. They perched there for a short while before flying off.

A small Muntjac deer appeared in my next-door neighbours' garden and looked through the adjoining gate, again while I was enjoying the garden and the weather one afternoon. We had all thought my neighbour had been hallucinating!

There is a great deal of symbolism in animals and at times what kind of animal or bird presenting itself to you can have greater knowledge, information and understanding than you realise. Most ancient cultures have understood this, but a lot of us sadly have moved away from that knowing which we all still have, but do not recognise and so do not remember.

"When one door closes another door opens but we often look so long and regretfully upon the closed door that we do not see the one that has opened for us"
Alexander Graham Bell

Disguised Magic

About 3 years before I began my formal training as a Medium, I went for a reading in Clacton. Amongst other things, the lady told me that 'You hear Spirit, and you hear very clearly'. I thought this must be wrong as I certainly did not believe that I heard unidentified voices in my head or otherwise. She then went on to say that I would be working on platform, which is a form of public demonstration of Mediumship. Mediumship is where a person believes they can communicate with those who have passed to the Spirit World. I was most indignant at this and adamant that that was never likely to happen.

About 18 months after this I went for another reading with a lady in Ely near Cambridge and half-way through the reading, she said 'I am being told that you hear Spirit, and you hear very clearly….' I replied 'I don't think so' but she insisted that that was what she was being told. She then went on to say that 'You will be working on Platform…' Again, I said I couldn't see myself doing that as I was not one to put myself in such a situation. She then said that this wasn't the first time I had been told this, to which I had to reply and agree that it wasn't. She then went on to say, 'When you hear it a third time then you will know the time is right!

She also confirmed that I had been allowed to do the Reflexology and the Reiki to build my confidence. She also said that I would be teaching and again this was being given to me to build my confidence so that when I did platform work it would be easier... I then said that there was a difference to speaking in front of a class with a lesson plan and knowing the subject to doing platform work where there is no script! She was adamant that it was being given to her in this way and that I would be told it again.

I vowed there and then never to have another reading. This is the rebellious side of me.

Another 18 months further on and a lady rang me out of the blue and said she lived in the next village, she was networking and wondered if I fancied meeting up and having a chat and so we agreed to meet in a local tea shop.

At some point the lady mentioned a Medium who worked at the other end of town. My curiosity got the better of me and she gave me the number of a Medium called Ann. I knew the name because my Mother had been a great advocate of the Mediumship evenings held locally, and Ann would organise them. Any way I completely forgot that I had vowed never to have another reading and so made an appointment and went along.

Half way through the reading and Ann suddenly said 'Mum tells me that you hear from Spirit and you hear very clearly' The look on my face must have been a picture as I realised what was coming next and sure enough she then said 'This isn't the first time you have been told this… but now you know the time is right' Well you could have knocked me over as each Medium had the same message, had used the same words and had said it as a follow on, but none could have known what the other had said…. so it must have come from Spirit. The next part of the message was that there was a Circle starting that evening and Mother wanted me to take part. I said okay I would attend.

Getting outside as reality set in, I began to wonder what I had done by saying yes, and how I was going to explain it to my husband. I put the thought out that when he asked me where I was going that I could find the right words and be able to say them in the right way. But I was amazed yet again because he didn't even ask.

In the circle that evening we did Ribbon readings and the lady I read for took everything I said and like most things if you do well you want to do more.

I stayed with that circle run by Heather Cremer for about 18 months and by that time realised I needed more and again asked that the next part of my development be made obvious. It didn't take long as I was already booked to go and see Tony Stockwell perform Mediumship at Colchester. Part way through the evening, he told the audience that he had a Centre in Wickford and so I thought to myself that I would look into classes there, not even knowing where Wickford was in relation to where I lived. It is only about 45 minutes from Halstead and so booked on a course.

Interestingly enough I have never heard from the messenger who gave me Ann's details and I couldn't find her in the phone book either. I even drove round the village where she said she lived, but nothing would jog my memory as to where she said she lived and from that day to this our paths have never crossed again. Wherever she came from… I owe her a huge debt of thanks for sending me to Ann and again changing my path towards my destiny.

"There are no mistakes, no coincidences. All events are blessings given to us to learn from"
Elizabeth Kubler-Ross

Numbers Magic

I cannot count the times that numbers have played a significant part in my life. Giving me guidance and help when I have asked for it.

I had a difficult choice one afternoon as to whether I should go to a meeting the following evening. It wasn't necessary that I be there, and as certain things had become difficult between some members of the group, I was struggling to motivate myself into going. I knew that if I started missing the sessions then it would be more difficult for me to pick up with them again, but the constant undercurrent of bad feeling was spoiling what should have been an enjoyable couple of hours and turning it into a chore.

I was entering Halstead where I lived at about 5pm and the traffic was building up and so my thoughts drifted to the following evening… I put the thought out… 'if I should not go to the meeting then I want to have 7, 77 and 777 brought to me before I go to bed tonight'… the very next car that came towards me had the number plate N7 **** and the car behind it was EX77 *** or something similar… I was surprised to say the least and waited for the next car to come along… but the number plate had no 7's in it at all. Traffic started moving and so I drove the rest of the way home.

Later on, that evening, I was reading a book while my husband was watching TV. I suddenly looked up from my book and on the television was an advert for a glass company and the telephone number was 0800 777 ***… Needless to say I didn't go to the meeting. The group soon disbanded anyway, but I was saved from being caught up in the bad feeling which ensued.

"We do not want riches, we want peace and love"
Red Cloud

Spirit Guide Magic – Red Cloud

I was taking part in a Spirit Guide workshop down in Waltham Abbey and on this day a Red Indian stepped forward… I could smell his sweaty body and there was a faint smell of wood smoke. His hands were worn and quite rough and his eyes although were set in an old face sparkled with a youthfulness. He identified himself by name as Chief Red Cloud.

I knew that famous medium Estelle Roberts was his channel for many years and it was difficult for me to accept him as a Guide for me or that he should grace me with his presence at all. I remember Tracy Higgs saying well why not? My thought went out 'if that was you today Red Cloud then show me a baby deer.' I do not ask for the usual but it has to be relevant and so it was that I was driving home that night and I liked to drive through Epping. I was just coming through a part of Epping Forest and up to a junction when… as I turned left to go towards Epping town there standing on the side of the road was a small deer, on it's own and as I drove past it, it just stood and stared as my car went past. I guess that my question was answered.

This was not the first time Red Cloud had been to me, but it was the first time I had been given his name.

The first time we met was when I had been on another Spirit Guide workshop with Natalie Walker at the Tony Stockwell Studios in Wickford. It was a day workshop and although I had an Indian Guide come to me, he was much younger and there was no communication whatsoever and so I left a little dejected and a little disappointed that nothing had materialised.

I returned home and forgot about my disappointment as the evening wore on, and indeed by the time I went to bed had pretty much put the day out of my thoughts as nothing much had happened.

About 2am I decided to sleep in the middle bedroom as my husband's snoring was keeping me awake and no sooner had I pulled the quilt up and settled myself down then the quilt was pulled back and beside the bed stood a Native American Indian. He was in full headdress and stretched out his hand to take mine.

I knew I wasn't asleep and as I took his hand and swung my feet over the side of the bed, I expected my feet to rest upon floorboards, but my bare feet sank into fresh grass. The room became fresh air and as we walked, I could see to my left a lake with water so still and clear it mirrored the surrounding countryside and sky. I estimated it to be late afternoon and as we walked beneath pine trees. I could see amongst the pine trees that there were teepees and people milling around. No-one took any notice of us, but it seemed not because they couldn't see us, but because we were nothing out of the ordinary.

There was a faint smell of wood smoke and the air apart from this was clear, sweet, and very fresh. It was quite warm with a slight breeze and I was comfortable walking through the village.

Pretty soon we came to the largest tepee and the Chief lifted back the hide which covered the entrance. As we entered the tepee it was quite dark, and it took a little while for my eyes to adjust to my surroundings. My feet were now walking on animal hide and fur and in the middle of the tepee was a fire and there were two women cooking and talking as we entered. They acknowledged the Chief and he them… he took off his head dress and hung it on a bare tree trunk with bare branches which stood in the corner… presumably to keep it pristine as indeed it was. He then beckoned me to sit down on the floor and we talked for a while… I cannot remember what about… I remember looking up at one point to see where the smoke was going only to see a hole in the top of the tepee and a dark night sky filled with stars beyond. There was also a dark moon. Very significant!

I was eventually escorted out of the tepee and we walked back the way we had come and the next thing I remember is that I got back into bed and rolled over. I remember waking up in the morning and knowing something special had occurred.

I know that I was not dreaming and yet there was something surreal about the whole incident. I didn't ask his name or at least I don't remember and if I did then it was forgotten to me before I woke.

The third time we met was a couple of years later when I was sitting in a trance circle in Cheshunt. I was resting in the afternoon as I did before travelling down and no sooner had I closed my eyes than a Native American stood beside the sofa. I recognised him as the man who had been to me and taken me to his village and as the man who had identified himself as Red Cloud. I then said to him… If you are indeed Red Cloud then you need to prove it to me so that there can be no mistake on my part. I was still struggling with why he should come to me… no sooner had I thought this then he disappeared as quickly as he had appeared. I remember thinking… oops.

I drove down to Cheshunt that evening and there was a group of about 8 of us… One of the men went first and then Kimberley took to the chair. The purpose of trance is for you to sit in an altered state of consciousness and to allow Spirit to draw close and to overshadow or to control your words and actions… no sooner had Kimberley sat in the chair then the energy changed, and I knew Red Cloud had arrived. The usual questions were asked by the other members of the group… such as 'Are you a relative for someone in the room', which received no response then Justin asked 'Are you a guide for someone in the room'. Straight away Kimberley sat forward and pointed to me... She seemed to grow in stature and her energy was very overwhelming. Justin then asked if he was a Native American because by now one or two members of the group were tuning in and were seeing and feeling who it was. I was saying nothing at this point. Kimberly raised her hand and pointed at me. Someone then asked if he had a message for me... again Kimberley sat further forward and in a deep booming voice said, 'Trust and Believe'. I then asked him a couple of questions and then he left as soon as he had arrived, and Kimberley's awareness came back to the room.

Justin then asked if I had known him before tonight as he seemed ****** off and he wouldn't like to meet this Guide when he was upset. I then told the group what had happened that afternoon and that Red Cloud had every right to be 'upset'!!! Red Cloud has been with me on and off since then.

Another time we met was when I was on a Trance weekend down in Kent with Medium Glynn Edwards. I was in meditation to meet a guide and once again Red Cloud stepped forward and during the meditation, I knew he was giving me answers to questions I hadn't even asked yet... amazing. I then had a conversation with my daughter during the lunch break and gave her the information I had been given in the morning. She was asking me the questions that I had been given the answers to in the meditation.

Our understanding of time is man made and linear. The Universe does not recognise time like that, so things do not always happen in an order we can comprehend. The Universe also knows what you need and not what you want… it hears what you mean and not what you say too.

Another meeting was when I was in meditation at home and Red Cloud gave me a Lotus Flower and I commented on the fact that I didn't realise that Lotus Flowers were native to America. To which he replied, 'This one was grown in Spirit' I am truly blessed to have Red Cloud pop in and out as he does because it is usually with some sort of understanding and massive learning for me.

"The greatest gift of life is Friendship and I have received it"
Hubert H. Humphrey

Dear Friend Magic

I was in meditation at Heathers circle in the December of 2006 and I was shown a photograph of my daughter's godfather at my daughter's christening, He said during the mediation that he made a promise on that christening day to look after my daughter and that he intended to keep his promise – it upset me quite a bit at the time because my daughter was 8 months pregnant. But Heather said it was his way of saying everything would be alright even if there was a problem with her pregnancy.

The 8th of January 2007 was a Monday and my daughter started into labour. Monday came and went with her visiting hospital but being sent home.

On the Tuesday I went to see her and to do some Reflexology to help her relax. While I was massaging her feet, I suddenly became aware of a female energy. I told my daughter this and she asked if it was Nan? But I knew the energy I was picking up was much younger and told her so. She then asked if the energy was connected to the house as she had only just moved in. Again, I had to say that it did not feel like that. I felt that the energy was very young. Our attention was then distracted, and it was only as I was going home that evening that I put the thought out that if the baby was to be a girl then could I have it confirmed in some way. This would be great learning for me and would boost my confidence in my own understanding

When I got home, I took a look at my emails as I was to be at the hospital the next day. My daughter was to be taken in if nothing had happened by the next morning.

The first email that came up was from someone called Darcie and in the subject was 'thanks for everything'. I knew if the baby was a girl my daughter was going to call her Darcie. I immediately called my daughter and told her the baby is a girl. She did not believe it because all the way through her pregnancy it had been thought that the baby was a boy. I was adamant that the female energy had been the baby and that the email although it was spam, was the confirmation that I had been asking for.

Wednesday came and we all went to the hospital and I was in the delivery room with my daughter and her partner as well as the midwife. The conversation came around as to what baby might be and my daughter told the midwife that everyone thought it was a boy, but Mum was insisting on it being a girl…the midwife looked at the monitor and said she thought it was a boy by it's heartbeat…but again I held on to the belief that I had been given the understanding that the baby was a girl.

A little while later and my daughter asked who was in the room and I knew her Godfather had appeared at the foot of the bed and I remembered the meditation I had in December and I knew things were about to go wrong… he came and stood next to me and I knew in the moment that it would be alright. Indeed, things did go wrong, and my daughter was to be taken for emergency surgery. I knew that Neville, her Godfather then went down with her to have an emergency caesarean. In fact, everything turned out really well and my daughter had a beautiful baby girl who they named Darcie.

About 5 weeks after Darcie was born, I decided that things had settled down nicely and I would go and tell my daughter about the meditation I had had in circle and what I knew of Neville in the delivery room.

I rang her and agreed to go round for lunch and after being there a little while I explained what I wanted to tell her and when I got to the part where I had been shown the photograph of Neville at the christening, she took a deep breath in, but insisted that I carry on. When I had finished my story, she then said, 'Now come with me'.

We went into the laundry room and on top of the washing machine sat the very photograph I had been shown in the meditation. My daughter explained to me that she had gone into the laundry room in the morning and she had picked up what she thought was a piece of paper, but in actual fact was the photograph. She couldn't understand how it had come to be there as any photographs were still packed away in the attic. My daughter and her partner had only moved into their cottage days before Darcie was born and they had not unpacked a lot of the boxes as yet.

I explained that the Spirit World can and do move things and that Neville obviously knew that I was going round that day and had prepared the way for us to believe that he was still looking after us.

Neville has come through many times over the years with help and guidance when I have needed it, especially if it involves my daughter and her children.

> *"Do not dwell in the past, do not dream of the future, concentrate the mind on the present moment"*
> Buddha

Buddha Magic

I have been very fortunate within my career to be in a position of mentoring others, not just when I worked in the corporate world as a Manager, but also within my mediumship.

I was running a 6-month course on Mediumship in Waltham Abbey and for my birthday the students bought me a statue of Buddha which stands about 3 feet high. I brought it home and placed it in the fireplace hearth in my sitting room… it was a perfect fit and everyone who sees it comments on its magnificence.

The following day I placed some bamboo plants next to him and a couple of elephant ornaments which we have and lit candles to welcome him into our home. Later that evening I was reading a book sitting next to my husband who was watching the television. I looked up from my book and I actually saw the Buddha move his hands apart and then bring them together again.

My husband was still watching the TV and I gave thanks for the experience I had just had. I believe it was Buddha's way of acknowledging my welcome and that he was happy to be there.

"Nature does not hurry, yet everything is accomplished"
Lao Tzu

Garden Buddha Magic

I was sitting in the garden visualising what it would be like to have a Summerhouse to do classes in and where I would put another Buddha which had been given me at the end of another course I had run.

I was deliberating as to whether he would go inside or outside even though he was a garden ornament, when my Son-in-Law pulled up in his van with one of his employees to measure how big the garden was and where I would like a Summerhouse to go. This had come about after a brief conversation some weeks earlier over dinner.

Needless to say, the timing was perfect, and the Buddha sits in the garden to the side of the door.

> *"Miracles do not, in fact, break the laws of Nature"*
> C S Lewis

Animal Magic

Jasper was a cat who just wandered in one day as a kitten and never really went away again. As time went on and it was obvious that no one wanted to claim him, I took responsibility for feeding him and taking care of his general wellbeing. He was such an old soul and loved meditation, sitting beside me whenever I sat. He never killed anything and indeed struggled to catch even a butterfly.

He became ill towards the end of his life and we eventually had to have him put to sleep. I was lost for a few days without him and 3 days after his passing I was sitting in the garden and on the phone to my daughter when I said that I just needed a sign to let me know that he had crossed over alright.... no sooner were the words out of my mouth when a white feather drifted from the sky and landed at my feet.

The vets sent me a card of condolence and on the front was a picture of a Forget-Me-Not flower and I vowed that when the Summerhouse was finished, I would put Jasper's ashes beside the door and plant some Forget-Me-Nots over the top. I did not have any in the garden and thought it would be a way of acknowledging how much I missed him and how much he had meant to me.

However, Jasper had other ideas because no sooner had the Summerhouse been finished then some Forget-Me-Nots popped up in a different part of the garden, which was in fact the spot he used to lie down and stretch out. This happened to be right next to where Geraldine my rabbit had her hutch.

So needless to say, both Jasper and the Forget-Me-Nots ended up in a different part of the garden, but in the right place after all.

"Praying privately in churches, I began to discover that Heaven was my true home and also that it was here and now, woven into this Life"
Lionel Blue

Career Direction Magic

I often like to sit in empty churches as I find the energy very special and very powerful. This one particular day I was sitting in a delightful little country church in the village of Brent Eleigh.

I was at a crucial time in my life as I had qualified as a complementary therapist the previous year and knew that I did not want to be a Corporate Accounts Manager for the rest of my working career. I had been asking for guidance and had started my own business and was working outside office hours and had built up a good clientele, but found that I still felt unsettled.

As I sat in the quiet of the church listening to the sounds of birds outside, I realised that although I kept asking for guidance, nothing seemed to be happening.... so I sat quietly and once more put the thought out that if my career was to change then I needed something to let me know that I was on the right track… I then promised not to ask anymore.

My mobile phone rang, and it was Nikki from the Lifeforce Centre in Colchester offering me a job as Assistant Tutor on the next Reflexology Course. I could not believe it! I hadn't even had to wait for the answer.

I have found that if you hold onto something so tight, the Universe cannot work with the energy produced by your thoughts and emotions. In the moment I had let the thought go and the energy went out and came back, a bit like when you are trying to remember someone's name and you cannot quite recall it. It is only when you forget you are trying to remember it and your mind is then taken up by new thoughts and experiences and so the name drops into your mind and you remember.

> *"We go to the grave of a friend saying, 'A man is dead'. But Angels throng about him saying 'A man is born'"*
> Henry Ward Beecher

White Feather Magic

I cannot count the number of white feathers I have received in acknowledgment or as a form of guidance to help me make a decision when I have been unsure of which way to go. I have over the years kept them all, but I have also noticed that quite often they are with me for a while, but then disappear. This is perfectly right for me as I believe that if they are there for healing or for help with a situation and that healing is finished and the situation is over then the feather disappears along with the issue.

The one White Feather that I would like to share with you here appeared one day when I nearly denied myself an incredible opportunity for learning.

I had been qualified as a Reflexologist for about 3 years and had booked on a post graduate day for Reflexology within Palliative care. Palliative care is for those people who are terminally ill with Cancer.

My Mother had passed with Cancer a few months earlier and although I had been drawn to do the course, on the morning I was due in London to take it, I was starting to have second thoughts. Anyway, I made my way to the train station and caught a train to London. I then made my way to the underground.

I was standing on the underground platform and the anxiety was building and I remember thinking that if I turned round now and retraced my footsteps and caught the next train back home, I could be there by late morning.

However, someone else had other ideas because as I stood there about to pick up my bag, I noticed something blowing along the platform several yards away. At a point directly in front of me it stopped and changed direction and blew 3 yards or so towards me and stopped at my feet. It was a White Feather and so I picked the feather up and put it in my pocket and continued to the workshop.

I had the most amazing day and learnt so much. If it had not been for that feather, I do believe that I would have returned home early and missed the healing and learning that came along with the day.

White feathers are commonly acknowledged as being signs from loved ones who have passed over to the world of Spirit and also a sign that an Angel has drawn near to give a sign of comfort, encouragement and love to those who need it and when they need it.

"How people treat you is their Karma. How you react is yours"
Wayne Dyer

Karmic Magic

One evening while at home, I needed some milk and so I decided to walk down the town to the local supermarket to buy some. It was a lovely September evening, warm and balmy.

I reached the top of the Halstead High Street and the supermarket was half-way down the hill on the other side of the road. As I started to walk down the hill, I remember thinking what a lovely still evening it was and how very quiet it was. There were no people about and oddly enough no traffic.

Anyway, I continued on my way and a few minutes later just as I drew level with a gentleman's outfitters, I heard a voice say, 'Have you got any spare change?' The doorway to the shop was set back and a young man was sitting with his back against the door, only visible as I drew level with the doorway.

The young man was in his mid-twenties and was dressed rather dishevelled but seemed rather clean. He wore a jacket over jeans and a shirt and a woollen hat on his head.

I opened my purse to have a look and the young man said that he needed to catch the next bus back to Clacton but needed some change as he did not have enough money for the fare. I only had a five-pound note which back in 2002 was quite a lot of money for me and more than what was needed for the fare. I explained that I only had the five-pound note and that I was going to get some milk and I would stop by on my way back from the supermarket and would give him some change then.

I carried on and crossed the road and again wondered at there being no traffic.

Having bought the milk I came out and crossed back over the road and as I drew level with the young man again, I opened my purse to give him some change only to realise that I had just given the change I had when I paid for the milk and that I only had the five pound note left. I did not hesitate however and gave the young man the note. He was reluctant at first, but once I insisted, he then said, 'I will take the five pound if I may recite you a poem?' I agreed with the exchange and he recited me a poem, which alas I cannot remember now, but I do remember thinking at the time how beautiful it was and feeling that something special was taking place.

After he finished, I said that the words of the poem were just beautiful, and I thanked him for them. He then explained that he had written the poem when he was a child and he had won an award with it... I said I was not surprised and once again thanked him for sharing such a moment. He then thanked me for the money and said 'God bless you' I then left him still sitting in the doorway.

As I walked back up the High Street, I remember feeling a little strange, but comforted somehow with what had happened. There was still no-one around and no traffic.

Once I got back home, I told my daughter about what had happened, and she just laughed at the fact that I had been conned out of five pounds and took great delight in telling me that Halstead does not have beggars and that there was no direct bus to Clacton and that I had been well and truly had.

I reflected on what she had said and have done many times since and have come to the conclusion that something special happened that evening and that some sort of karma had been realised and that I was grateful for having the opportunity of paying back some sort of debt and being in the right place at the right time to understand it as such.

"Whatever you do may seem insignificant, but it is most important that you do it"
Mahatma Gandhi

Passing Stranger Magic

I had rented rooms in Halstead High Street and had asked my daughter to help me take a glass display cabinet down so that I could display various items that I had for sale.

As we got in the van to take the cabinet down, I put the thought out that I would be grateful for a parking space outside the shop. As we approached the High Street outside the shop not only was one parking space free, but the space was big enough for about 3 cars. We parked the van and I ran to the shop to open all the doors so that we had a clear run through as the cabinet was very heavy.

Before I went back outside again, I put the thought out that we may need some additional help as the cabinet was heavy and I wasn't sure if I would be able to help lift it. I went back outside and saw my daughter lifting the cabinet out of the back of the van with a young strong man on the other end of the cabinet… he had parked his van behind my daughter's van and had seen what she was off loading and had asked if he could help.

He was amazing and took the cabinet all the way through the shop to the room that I was renting. We both thanked him, and I put the thought out that it would be nice if something good could happen to him to repay the debt energetically.

I am sure that the Universe which had answered my calls for help would now answer my call to action to give this man a reward in some way.

I always ask that something good happen for people that have let me into traffic, or have helped or been courteous to me in some kind of way.

> *"Faith is taking the first step even when you do not see the whole staircase"*
> Martin Luther King Jnr

Tarot Card Magic

My first pack of Tarot cards was bought for me by a friend who knew that I was showing an interest in such things. However, no matter how hard I tried and how many times I read the instruction manual, I could not get the meaning of the cards to stay in my memory.

Six or Seven years later I bought myself a different pack of cards and they arrived one day when I was quite busy, so I didn't get a chance to open them when they came. That evening I was due at the local Primary School for a pamper evening where I was to do 1-2-1 readings and put the new cards in my bag with the idea that should I not be busy then I could open the cards and look at them.

I arrived at the venue and set my table up and had about 15 minutes before the doors opened. I took out the new set of cards and was quite excited when I looked at them. They were bright and colourful, and the images seemed to connect with me.

Inside the pack was a printed card with an illustration of a 5-card spread on it and it seemed to be relevant to current lifestyles? Just as I was shuffling the cards, my intention was to do a 5 card spread for myself, one of the ladies who was organising the event came over and said, 'We have a few minutes before the doors open and I see you have some Tarot cards, I have never had a Tarot reading before, would you read them for me?'

Before I knew it, I heard myself say 'Yes of course.'

I put the thought out to the Universe that, 'You have dropped me in it now, you had better help me out' I then explained to the lady that I had only just got the cards today and that I do not usually read cards and so if she let me use the 5 card spread as illustrated, then I would give it a go… at the end of the reading she said that I had been spot on with the information and that if that was the first time I had read for anyone then I should carry on. By this time the doors had opened, and my first client arrived and saw that I was reading cards and wanted a Tarot reading… I did Tarot readings all night and that was the start of my offering to give 1-2-1 Tarot readings.

I do need a push now and again and this certainly was a big push, but Spirit does know best.

> *"What's in a name? That which we call a Rose by any other name would smell as sweet"*
> William Shakespeare

Spirit Name Magic

Psychic Medium Tracy Higgs, who had her own Centre in Waltham Abbey, was running a course in Dublin Ireland. She asked me to go with her to help assess her students on the last weekend of a Mediumship course. This was in the Autumn of 2014.

On the Friday evening when we were having dinner, Tracy mentioned that she felt my Mother was near. My Mother had been passed some 13 years or so, but Tracy kept getting interrupted by my Mother drawing close. I explained that mother's family were Irish and so she was probably relishing the fact that I was there... she also likes to pop in when I am teaching or doing something different.

Tracy finally managed to enjoy her evening and Mother left her alone. However, my Mother was never one to take no for an answer or to be ignored and she proved this the very next morning.

Tracy and I approached the room where we were to meet her students and on the door the Hotel had put a name which read 'Higgins' and not 'Higgs'. I had to laugh and explained to Tracy that my Mother's maiden name had been

Higgins. Tracy's only comment was that my Mother was persistent!!

Funnily enough it was at another event Tracy was organising that my Mother again showed her remarkable way of letting me know that she was with me and this time it was in March 2017. Tracy had organised a Spiritual weekend at Pontins Pakefield in Suffolk. I had been thinking of my Mother much of the journey, but especially the last part. As I neared the venue, I fondly remembered spending my early childhood here as my Father was born and lived in the area until he joined the RAF in the late 1930's when he was posted to an airfield near Walsall, Birmingham and met my Mother. They later returned to Suffolk and even though we moved away my fathers family still lived in the area.

As I drove up to the gate I opened the passenger window, as that was the side the security man was standing on. Before I could ask him where I should be going, he leant into the window and said, 'Let me guess you are one of Miss Higgins group.' I didn't correct him, just laughed to myself and drove to where he had directed.

> *"One thing to remember is to talk to the animals. If you do, they will talk back to you. But if you don't talk to the animals, they won't talk back to you, then you won't understand, and when you don't understand you will fear, and when you fear you will destroy the animals, and if you destroy the animals, you will destroy yourself"*
> Chief Dan George – Tsleil-Waututh (1899-1981)

Australian Horse Magic

My husband and I went on holiday in 2010 to visit my Sister in Adelaide Australia. I had not seen her for 39 years, because she and her family had moved to Australia in 1970 when I was still a child.

My daughter had been having digestive problems, immense pain and passing out after eating. The local surgery had been slow in my opinion with finding out what the real problem was. On the day we were due to fly, my daughter collapsed again, and my husband said to me that we did not have to go, we could stay and support her. However, my daughter rallied round and came to see us off. Her partner assured me that he would ring the surgery and insist that they do something about it.

On the plane my husband and I were talking about my daughter and I assured him that if my daughter did not get the help she needed by the time we arrived back in the UK, I was prepared to sit in the surgery until I saw her Doctor and until I had some answers as this had been going on for a year now and my Grand-daughter was witness to her mother's pain and trauma.

My husband did say that the Doctor would not be able to tell me anything as all information would be confidential… I then said that I did not want any personal information I just wanted the Doctor to answer a question I had, and that question was, 'Can you tell me that my daughter does not have an ulcer, stomach cancer or some other serious condition that they were not diagnosing?' No investigation was being carried out and the antacid medication was clearly doing no good.

The day after we arrived in Australia, I heard that my daughter was to have a scan at the hospital… that was to be a week later.

On the day of the scan my husband and I were to go to Kangaroo Island which is just off the coast of South Australia… my Niece and her Boyfriend would be with us. I sat in the garden before we were due to leave and put the thought out to my Mother, Neville and my Brother Tony to be with my Daughter on this day as I couldn't be there.

We missed the Ferry to Kangaroo Island and had to wait until the next one, so with some free time we took a short ride to the beach and on the way back up the track to the main road, I saw a field with 2 horses in it, they were moving towards the fence and I asked that the car be stopped so that I could get out… I walked to the fence and stood and waited for the horses to reach me... I hadn't noticed the third horse as it was a Shetland and the grass verge from the car to the fence was rather tall, and so the Shetland could not be seen from the car.

All three horses came to the fence for me to stroke... I suddenly had the idea that everything with my daughter would turn out well and that the solution to her medical condition was going to be resolved. I thanked the horses and the Universe for the understanding and it suddenly occurred to me that what I was looking at was a Chestnut Mare – my Mother, a Bay Stallion – Neville and the Shetland – my Brother who passed when he was only three. I still look at the photograph which my Niece took of me and the horses and give thanks for the way the Universe always gives me the reassurance that I ask for.

My daughter it turns out had gallstones and had her gallbladder removed only a couple of weeks later.

> *"A Dragonfly to remind me even though we are apart*
> *Your Spirit is always with me forever in my heart"*
> Angelina LaFera

Australian Dragonfly Magic

On another day out in Australia with my Nephew and his wife I had the feeling that my Mother was around and so asked that if it was her then to bring me a Dragonfly to confirm.

We met my Nephew and his wife at a place called Victor Harbour and I told Angela about my thoughts to my Mother and she then said that she had a Dragonfly on her bracelet... I acknowledged it but did say that my Mother would make it a bit more obvious, because she would. My Mother was a very determined woman, and I knew there would have to be something more dramatic in her confirmation.

We had walked across a short causeway to a small outcrop of land called Granite Island which is a Nature Reserve and once at the top had some amazing views. We climbed for about an hour or so and stood looking out over the sea... and just as we were about to come down, both Angela and I had forgotten about the Dragonfly, all of a sudden out of nowhere came a Dragonfly... amazingly the Dragonfly followed us nearly all the way to the causeway. Angela could hardly believe it, but I knew Mother would not let me down.

"Don't be afraid to change.
You may lose something good, but you may also gain something better"
Anonymous

Moving House Magic

My husband had been talking about moving to a new house for about three years, but I was reluctant. I had a network of friends and family around me and my business was based in Halstead, Essex. While my husband was working away, I also felt moving to a new house on my own would prove to be too big a task and any way I loved my house and my life just as it was.

However, in late 2015, I knew my husband was thinking of extending his contract abroad and as I asked The Universe for peace of mind with this, a veil kind of lifted and I knew that I should move, with help or without it.

My husband came home on leave in early February 2016 and I had booked for us to look at a couple of properties. I put the thought out before we went to look at them that if one of the houses we would be looking at was right for us then 'bring me a Dragonfly within the boundary of the property.' I remember thinking that if it was a real one then I would really be impressed as it was the wrong time of year… but I was open to how it would come nonetheless.

The first house we looked at was an old cottage with very low ceilings and was totally inappropriate for our family home. The second was in better condition and had lovely proportions, but the garden was not right for us.

The day before my husband was due to fly abroad, we had arranged to pick our eldest Granddaughter up in the early afternoon and we were having a bit of lunch in Sudbury, Suffolk before collecting her. We were only in this particular café because the week before our Granddaughter had insisted on going in for lunch because she had been in with a friend from school and it was now very nice. Reluctantly we had agreed but had found that it had changed hands recently and it was in fact quite nice.

Anyway, my husband and I had finished our lunch this particular day and were thinking about making a move to go and pick Darcie up when we received a phone call from my daughter to say that they were on the way to A&E because Darcie had fallen over and cut her head open. As we sat there, I said to my husband that if we were now seriously considering moving to a new house then maybe we should put our name down with an Estate Agent. His response was that we had all the time we needed now that our plans had changed.

There were two Estate Agents either side of the café, but I looked over my husband's shoulder and out of the window to the Estate Agents across the road and said I wanted to go there. He reiterated that we could go anywhere as we had plenty of time, but I was already up and on the move.

As we stood in front of the Estate Agents window, I looked at a picture of a property on the top row and said, 'I want to go and look at that one,' pointing at the picture. My husband's response was that he had already shown me that property 2 or 3 times and each time I had said that I didn't like it. 'Even so,' I said, 'I want to go and look at that one'. I had no doubt and in fact didn't even glance at the other pictures in the window. My husband, a little exasperated, said 'fine, fine, fine' and headed for the door.

We couldn't get to see the property before my husband had to leave for abroad, and so I made the appointment to view the property the day after he left.

My daughter came with me and as we pulled up outside, she commented on the fact that it wasn't somewhere she had thought I might like.

We went inside and looked around and the house had so much potential I could hardly contain myself. We then had a look round the garden, and I could see an extension in my mind and how each room could look.

Once we were back inside again the Estate Agent asked if we would like another look around and I said that I did. My daughter and I discussed my ideas and what I thought could be done with the property. Back down in the kitchen with the Estate Agent, I began putting my boots back on. As I bent down to do them up, I noticed a packet of tea on the worktop. The owners had partially moved out and so the worktop was clear except for a kettle and this packet of tea.

I asked my daughter what the packet of tea was called to which she heaved a heavy sigh and said 'You cannot buy a house on a packet of tea'… she knows me so well… I again repeated the question and said I was just asking for confirmation of the name. 'It is Dragonfly Tea' she said.

The Estate Agent just looked and said nothing. Needless to say, I bought the house and am very happy here. As I write this, we are waiting for the building work to start the extension.

> *"Goodbyes are not forever*
> *Goodbyes are not the end*
> *They simply mean I'll miss you*
> *Until we meet again"*
> Anonymous

Meditation Magic

I run a Thursday evening online meditation group, and although I sit with my eyes closed throughout, I don't actually do the meditation with them.

However, sometimes others seem to know best, and it was on a Thursday evening close to the 3rd anniversary of my Dad's passing and I had just been told that my first book was about to be published.

I had taken the group to a hammock hung between two trees at the edge of a beach. They could smell the sea air and feel the soft gentle breeze on their skin along with the warmth of the sun. As they looked up, they could see the blue sky flickering between the dark green leaves of the trees. The picture I was painting in my mind was of a tropical beach. I told them I would leave them there for a while, and they could either stay gently swaying in the hammock or get up and explore. Either way, I would call them back when it was time.

As I have said, I don't normally do the meditation with them, but all of a sudden, I was there in the hammock, looking up at the sky through the leaves and smelling the sea and listening to the waves gently lapping at the beach. The sun was warm and the breeze a delight. I could hear birds somewhere in the distance. I decided to get up and as I put my feet down, I saw a Hedgehog… I realised that I had no food for it and nothing to give to it, but just as quickly realised that it could find its own food and look after itself perfectly well.

I walked across the beach, the warm sand under my bare feet and stopped as the waves gently fell around my feet. The water was warm yet refreshing. I looked to my right and saw two people coming towards me, and as they came closer, I realised them to be my Mother and Father. They seemed a lot younger and blissfully happy together. They were hand in hand both were barefoot, and my Dad had his trousers rolled up to his knees. It took me aback because I don't remember them being this way. But it was lovely to see, and I am thankful to witness it. I walked towards them and as we met, we hugged each other, again not a memory of this world. In my mind, I thanked them for being there. There was someone else coming along the beach now. A tall slender man with dark reddish hair. I intuitively knew him to be my brother who I had never known as he had passed away at the age of three, long before I was born.

I told him how lovely it was to meet him at last and asked him if he loved the beach too. To which he replied, 'I don't have this as an earthly memory, so it is difficult for me to say,'. I thought, well that was a reasonable answer, and we had a hug anyway.

Over his shoulder, I then caught sight of a dear friend who is also in the Spirit World and who I have already mentioned in this book. I ran over and we hugged each other too. No words necessary here. And then who should I see standing on the beach, but Colin Fry and I went to him and thanked him for being here and for the connection we had when he was living.

As I stepped back and marvelled at these wonderful people who were all around me, I noticed a figure some way off in the distance, along the tree line. I knew who it was instantly and knew he wouldn't come to me and so I walked to him. He had the full Native American headdress on and the clothes to match. They were pristine as if his best gear or brand new. I hugged my guide and got quite emotional as I stepped back and thanked him for being there too and how lovely it was that they should all come to me in this way. He replied that I should never doubt that they were with me, supporting me and would continue to do so. By this point, I was beyond quite emotional, but I knew it was time to come back to the Meditation group and bring everyone including myself back to this reality.

Hedgehog – The spiritual meaning of Hedgehog, because I haven't forgotten about the Hedgehog... Open yourself to receive! What you have asked for is now manifesting. Follow through on your ideas and intuition – Awesome

SECTION THREE - Other Peoples Magic

"True friends are always together in Spirit"
L M Montgomery

I wanted to include in this book the magic that other people have experienced too, because it is not only me that can see and experience these things, but everyone else can too.

I have asked friends to contribute their thoughts and experiences and these are written here in their own words and in the way they have remembered them.

SALT LAMP Magic – Love Bel x

Do you remember I told you how my intuition 'sucked' because I chose that faulty Salt Lamp and it had a split in the wire? Well, we took it back to the shop yesterday to get it exchanged and the lady who owns the shop recognised us as soon as we walked in. I showed her the fault, and she apologised for it and chose another one for me. She checked it over herself and made sure it worked which it did. I thought that would be it, but then she said to us (good marketing ploy I guess), Have a look around the shop and if there is anything you want you can have 25% off for the inconvenience of having to come back. Kev said, 'What anything in the shop?' and she said 'Yes'. Well, we ended up buying another 3 Christmas presents that came within our budget (we'd liked the items before, but they were more than what we wanted to pay) and we got 25% off each item. We were really pleased and of course so was she because we bought more stuff. So, you see, it worked out well in the end.

BARN OWL Magic - Karen

This is an example of one of the most amazing 'magic moments' I have ever experienced.

My mother and I were extremely close, she was not only my mum, but my best friend and the one person I could always rely on. She would always be there to listen to my worries and troubles and she would never judge, even if she didn't agree with my perspective on an issue or if she didn't agree with something I had done/was about to do, she would give me her opinion and never said, 'I told you so' if my decision was the wrong one.

We were brought even closer together by a very abusive domestic home life and as much as she was my protector, I also felt I became hers. When, after over ten years of battling and living with Alzheimer's Disease she sadly passed away, it was the single worst moment and event of my life so far.

Over a month before Mum passed, I had a reading with Linda and asked her if she knew when mum's passing would be and Linda said all she could say about that was that the number 5 was significant.

In the days leading up to Mums passing Mum spent a lot of that time in bed and obviously with her advanced stage of Alzheimer's she had no idea what day it was, let alone what time of the year we were in, she also did not speak much at all. A few days prior to Mum's death she sat up in bed and in a loud and perfectly clear voice she said, 'I want to go to the other side on the 5th of December!'! I was absolutely shocked, shaken and amazed. I asked her to repeat what she just said, but the moment had passed, and she never spoke that way again.

Linda was a great comfort and help to me during this time and she advised me to write Mum a letter 'letting her go' as she felt Mum was only still here because she was worried how I would be once she had gone – a completely double-edged sword as I didn't want her to go, but I couldn't bear watching her suffering either. So, on the 2nd of December I wrote the letter to her, through buckets of tears.

Mum passed away on Saturday the 3rd of December.

On the Monday, the 5th of December, we began making the funeral arrangements. I couldn't help but think about the fact that this was the day Mum had said she wanted to be on the other side.

We visited the funeral directors and were told that it is quite unlikely that the funeral will be this side of Christmas and may end up being early in the new year – something none of us wanted. The lady in the funeral directors said she would enquire and call me later. We left and took a drive up to Marks Hall Estate with a view to seeing if they would be able to arrange a funeral tea. Marks Hall is a very special place for me as it is where mum and I spent many happy times, not just going around the grounds but also just sitting taking in the gardens, having a chat with a cup of tea. Brian, my partner, was driving, and I was in the passenger seat with my close friend Sue in the back as we drove up the long drive towards Marks Hall. It was mid-afternoon and although the scenery was beautiful it was also very bleak and very cold – it was a proper wintry landscape with a slight mist covering the ground low down, but ever so peaceful. As we drove along the straight road from the public car park to the Estate Office, I noticed I had a missed call from the funeral directors on my phone, so I immediately called them back. As the lady answered the phone and I said hello, to my left, out of the window was the most beautiful white barn owl in flight, literally alongside our car, going in the same direction and only about four feet away from us. I tapped Brian on the arm and pointed and he stopped the car to look. Whilst this was happening the lady from the funeral directors said, 'I was ringing to offer you a date for Mum's funeral service' - At that very moment the owl turned to the left and landed on a tree branch directly in line with where we were stopped – '22nd of December if that is suitable?' she said.

As she spoke the owl seemed to turn his head and look directly at me, in fact I would say more than look at me he seemed to look into me and in that moment, I truly believed it was a sign that Mum was with me. She was now flying free from all the constraints life had dealt her, and she was saying yes take that date. The date was also significant in that mum was born on the 22nd of July and I was born on the 22nd of March, so '22' was our lucky number!

I have never seen a wild barn owl in flight, in the daytime at Marks Hall or anywhere else, before or since. The whole experience is one that will remain with me forever and that in that moment, it gave me great comfort, knowing this was also the day my Mum had said herself that she wanted to be 'on the other side'.

HOUSE MOVE Magic - Jane

We were planning to move as a family from the Midlands to Essex. I really was not looking forward to the move but had to remain positive for the family.

I frequently saw my 'special' lady who predicted to me on one of my doubtful moments that the house we were going to move to would have a round window and the garden would have some form of topiary.

Eventually I found our current house and came to view it, I knew as soon as I walked in this was the house for us, despite not hitting my criteria and no round window! I wasn't really looking for a round window, but perhaps had it in the back of my mind because of what had been said!

On viewing the property, I realised looking at the property details that the picture of the advertised house was not the house I was viewing. Standing back on the road and looking at all the houses along the road, I then realised it was the house next door. The agent had obviously taken a photograph of the wrong house. The house next door had a circular window looking out on to the property we were intending to purchase!

Originally at the back of our house there were orchards, and the apple trees were annually pruned and shaped very neatly resembling lolly's on sticks. I think I was pleasantly surprised when I realised all that I had been told had come to fruition. It was not that I disbelieved my lady, but I felt it was more like reassurance and the right decision had been made to purchase the property and I would be happy here.

It's a daunting experience anyway moving so far from what you would call your home and leaving family not knowing a soul and wondering how it is all going to be. I felt my lady had kindly given me that special encouragement and confidence for the big transformation.

SHAMAN Magic - Sharon

I had been working on a Shamanism course which involved tuning into nature and journeying to meet power animals amongst other things. I had a tree in my garden which there was a problem with, so I felt I should take a picture of the Tree. The Tree was being cut down and as I gave healing to the Tree, I promised I would plant another tree as soon as I could.

When I looked at the photos of the Tree, I saw an image of a person...the longer I looked the more images I could see. There was an image of a wolf and a bear. I believe these were the Nature Spirits, Guardians and Protectors of the Tree.

At around the same time, I was using my deer skin drum that I had made for my Shamanic work and as I looked at the skin there was a very prominent wolf's head, a swan, a goat and a dolphin to name but a few.

Shamanism has certainly opened up my eyes to there being more to this world than we are used to seeing and understanding.

MOBILE PHONE Magic - Jess

I had just received a new mobile phone but wasn't happy with it and was sending it back. My eldest daughter was to have my old phone... which really wasn't that old and was now huffing and puffing and moaning that she would have to wait now for my new new phone to arrive so that she could then have my old phone, which I was still having to keep until the new new phone arrived. I hope you are keeping up.

She was huffing and puffing and moaning about how it was going to be days now before she could have my old phone, this continued for about an hour and a half, all the time I was trying to reload my information back onto my old phone. Which for some reason wouldn't work!

In exasperation and a lot of huffing and puffing on my part, I gave up and tried to download my information onto her old old phone and it downloaded straight away as did her information to my old phone. So, I then ended up with her old old phone, until my new phone arrived.

The Universe does work in extraordinary ways, for some of us at least – ha ha

Book Editing Magic - Carrie

I am Linda's virtual assistant and whilst I was proofreading this book I sent Linda a text message as I had a magical experience myself! I was visited by my Grandad (who is in spirit). I identified him by his smell that I was so used to smelling as a child. I welcomed him and said hello. He said "hello gal" back and encouraged me to take note of the song that was playing on Alexa. It was 'Praise You' by FatBoy Slim. My heart was beating so fast that I could hear it and it made me feel like I should be proud of my achievements and that my Grandad felt proud of me and wanted to praise me and that I must continue my work with Linda.

SECTION FOUR - And Finally

"The living Soul of man, once conscious of its power cannot be quelled"
Horace Mann

I don't have to ask for signs and reassurance anymore, because things happen around me all the time to encourage me and to bring me the understanding that I am completely supported and heard by the Universe. I know now that the Universe knows what I need even before I know that I need it myself.

Your Soul Energy is expansive, aware, joyful and intuitive. It is complete and is your extension of self. It will only ever give you the absolute truth because that is what unconditional love is and it communicates with the Universe on your behalf and for your highest good.

Know that you are communicating with the Universe, all day, every day, even if you do not realise it. Know that it is working continually to give you what you need and with unconditional love. Sometimes it is only with hindsight that we become aware of how the Universe guides us.

Trusting and believing will build confidence not only in the Universe, but in yourself too, through a sense of being worthy and this worthiness helps you to make better choices. Your spiritual evolution demands it.

I do hope you have enjoyed reading about the magic which is all around us and that you too have experienced it in your own way. If you haven't recognised it yet, then I do hope by reading this book you will begin to see the magic for yourself.

Magic is everywhere but sometimes we do not believe it because we do not look for it. Start by looking for it now, and don't forget the magic is inside of you too.

Peace, happiness, and Universal Magic to you all.

Linda

Printed in Great Britain
by Amazon